HENRY COTTON

My

Golfing Album

THE INCOMPARABLE THRILL OF DRIVING DOWN HILL : TEMPLE GOLF CLUB

HENRY COTTON

My Golfing Album

COUNTRY LIFE LIMITED LONDON

Published in 1959
by Country Life Limited
Tavistock Street London W C 2
Printed in Great Britain by
Balding & Mansell Ltd
London and Wisbech

TO DEAR TOOTS

We have climbed many a hill together, hand in hand, and you know, better than anyone else, what it means to be at the top of the golf game, but despite all the ups and downs of life, your helping hand has always been there!

Thanks a million!

LIST OF CONTENTS

My Golfing Album

My Golfing Album

HOW QUICKLY THE YEARS FLY!

How quickly the years fly! I look forward annually to the warmth of spring and summer and that clean smell of mown fairways, and then before I can say I have enjoyed them to the full, here I am looking forward to the next spring and summer, and in my excitement I forget I am steadily running out of time. Things are so arranged in this world by our Creator that whatever happens we all run out of time finally.

I have now gone fifty, which I suppose one day will be a sort of half-way mark in human life, but to-day it means that more than the best half has already gone; one can say that 'the future is behind one'. Anyway, I feel like doing some summing-up. When one is young, one seeks all the honours one can get, and there always seems to be time to obtain them, and then all of a sudden how grateful one becomes for what one has got — never mind what one missed.

My generation of golfers had the long years of World War II cut into their lives, but those of us who were spared, while, may be, having a regret at having missed chances to add to our laurels, can be thankful anyway.

I decided at one moment to stop playing in major golf tournaments, to rest on my laurels, but then I suddenly became aware that, while my well-wishing friends were giving me good advice, which I thought seemed sound common sense, about retiring from competitive golf, I did after all love golf very much. I love the competition, and the personal challenge a well-prepared course made to me, and I felt that if I could still play decently enough to be considered a competitor, not a passenger merely crowding the field, I would go on enjoying this sort of tough golf. While it is to me a sort of torture, it is that sweet sort of suffering which gives much satisfaction to the sufferer. Although past fifty, I realized that I could play within a stroke or two as well as I did twenty years previously if I felt really fit, and even if I did notice that my recuperative powers had diminished, provided that my heart was sound, I could still get a big kick out of playing against the young golfers.

At the same time I could test out some theories I had worked on since I was very young — namely, that my action was one which would not only last me all my life, but would produce satisfactory results when one-time rivals had dropped back on the golfing ladder.

I decided years ago that easy golf was a game of hands and arms, and that no trouble should be spared to build up the hands and arms, so that the club could be swung fast and truly. I felt then, as I still feel to-day, that many of the great champions are apt to overlook the fact that they have excessively strong hands, a grip like a vice in fact, and so they unconsciously mislead others when giving advice. They put the accent on other parts of the body, simply because their hands have never been a problem to them.

All I can say is that if you give Mr Jim Snooks Sam Snead's or my own hands, he will be almost scratch the next day, even using his own special sort of swing. In fact, I will go even further and say that his special sort of swing, which he and his teachers claim lets him down, is only so condemned because he tries somehow to cover up the weakness of his hands and fingers and make do with the muscles he has, which are non-golfing ones.

So in the following pages are comments on various points which I found interesting to golfers during discussions both on and off the course. Fifty years is not perhaps considered a great age, but I think that I have accumulated in that time some information which I can pass on to interest and entertain golfers everywhere. I have not tried to cover all the golf game nor the styles of all the great golfers I have seen in my lifetime — others better qualified than myself set about this task regularly — but I have tried to hit the various nails right on the head as they have come before me. I have not tried to set out any ordered sequence of chapters, such as driver to putter, which I have previously done in other books, but to flit about among my photographs and memories for ideas, and so I present:

My Golfing Album!

THE BEST THINGS IN LIFE

I SIMPLY have to put these lines in my album. They are not exactly words of golfing advice, which I set out to give, but all the same I feel I need not apologise for them, for they just about sum up life to me, as I am sure they will to many others who read them.

After all we are all three people in one: 'The person we think we are, the person others think we are, and the person we really are.'

'Youth is not a time of life—it is a state of mind. It is not a matter of ripe cheeks, red lips, and *supple knees*, it is a temper of the will, a quality of the imagination, a vigour of the emotions, a predominance of courage over timidity, of the appetite for adventure over love of ease. This often exists in a man of fifty more than in a boy of twenty.

Nobody grows old by merely living a number of years, people grow old only by deserting their ideals. Years wrinkle the skin, but to give up enthusiasm wrinkles the soul. Worry, doubt, self-distrust, fear and despair — these are the long, long years that bow the head and turn the growing spirit back to dust.

Whether 70 or 16, there is in every being's heart the love of wonder, the sweet amazement at the stars and the star-like things and thoughts, the undaunted challenge of events, the unfailing appetite for what next, and the joy and the game of life.

You are as young as your faith, as old as your doubt, as young as your self-confidence, as old as your fear, as young as your hope, as old as your despair.

So long as your heart receives messages of beauty, cheer, courage, grandeur and power from the earth, from man and from the *infinite*, so long you are young.

When the wires are all down and all the central place of your heart is covered with the snows of pessimism, than you are grown old indeed and *may God have mercy on your soul*.'

— AUTHOR UNKNOWN : quoted from *The Best Things in Life*, by Harry Hepner (B. C. Forbes Publishing Co.)

LET'S START

The beginning of the round of golf — even this takes a beginner time to learn. The simple act of teeing up the ball does not need two hands, after all, he finds.

The way I do it. Some golfers put the back of their hand on the ground so that they press the tee peg between their fingers and so get the same height of tee each time — the thickness of the hand is the measure. Not a bad idea!

BUILDING UP THE HEART OF THE GOLF SWING

From what I have seen of handicap golfers, very few ever experience that solid impact of the ball being struck in the centre of the club face, where the shaft vibrates in their hands. So many seem to brush away the ball, and it must feel dead, as if the clubhead cover had not been removed.

Players learn to go from A to B (top of the swing to end of follow-through) without ever building up the heart of the swing — i.e., the hitting area. Some exercises I have found which help are:

Hit the ball and swish the clubhead straight back immediately after impact — this teaches the player to hang on, as it puts a double strain on the wrists and forearms and keeps the head down.

Hit and stop, using the left arm and wrist as a buffer for the right hand's hit. I usually put over the feel of the hand action in these strokes by placing my right hand on the shaft, taking the place of the pupil's right hand, and then we swing the club together.

Remember that your hands cannot be too strong. I have never yet met a golfer whose hands were too strong. You see it is not the amount of practice which counts in golf — *it is how you practise*. If you want to succeed, exercise your hands and fingers with spring grips, heavy clubs, by doing press ups, hanging from a bar, squeezing a rubber ball, rolling up sheets of newspaper one-handed into tiny balls, beginning at one corner,

Here is a pupil doing his 'hit and stop' drill. All 'Cotton School' pupils will have worked on this drill, I trust with advantage, because it does put the maximum strain on the hands and arms.

I can hit the ball within 20 yards of my best possible efforts with my driver, using this action. The clubhead does not follow-through more than this. It is an exercise to fit into every practice session.

rolling up a weight on a stick, playing rapidly seven or more golf balls to get them into the air at one time; this is very good drill, and so on. They will all help your impact.

THE LATEST SECRET

The word 'secret', when mentioned in connection with the golf game, makes all golfers prick their ears, and everyone, from the very beginner who thinks the professional is 'holding one back' from him, to the near-champion, who still turns and twists in the hope of unearthing that something new, which will make him outshine the rest — all think this idea of a secret fascinating.

Following on Ben Hogan's 10,000 dollars-worth of 'secret', I read an amusing couple of paragraphs by Jimmy Hines, who followed Ben as professional at the Thunderbird Club in Palm Springs. Jimmy is quite a wit; I like this: 'There is only one theory on golf, but I have one, too, and that is that if fewer theories were tried, sounder golf would result. But why should I give the usual wrinkles the golf professional strings his pupils along with, when I have just decided to reveal the real secrets of the game? A sure-fire method is to take lessons

from at least half-a-dozen professionals, then sort it out yourself. If two heads are better than one, why not six? Besides, there is a variety and spice to all this which makes the game a real challenge. Instead of having the simple fundamentals grooved into an easy swing, that permits you to give full concentration to a particular type of shot you wish to play, you can reconstruct the picture a half-dozen times. If it does not quite come off, try "What's-his-name's" suggestion next time. You're sure to get it. In fact, you'll get it any number of times for years to come.

'Don't stay with one thought too long. It gets you in a rut. Have a little new theory ready once a month, week, or each hole if you prefer. You might try this one on the first tee to-morrow. Without thinking of anything else, "just stare at the back of the ball where you plan to hit it". Or you might give this one a whirl. "Clench your

Golf magazines in the 1920–30 period claimed these two swings as classical: Bobby Jones (LEFT), *Tommy Armour* (RIGHT). *In my eyes they are still right to-day. The left wrist under the shaft at the top is right for the vast majority of golfers — no danger of disc trouble in this method.*

it can be a tendency to drift to one side of the fairway or the other. Dai Rees was telling me that Sam Snead quick-hooked seven drives in 36 holes they once played together, which means (with eight short holes) one drive in every four. Some players tend to cut, others to hit the ball 'thin'. So, if a player all of a sudden cuts down his percentage of poor shots by doing some new-for-him action, then he might claim it as a 'secret', if it produced him a big success. But, as Jimmy Hines said: 'Don't stay with one thought too long: it gets you in a rut.' And this is what most amateurs' secrets become: they become ruts which are hard to get out of.

When I was asked during a lecture in the St Andrew's Hall, Glasgow, 'Did I believe in the forward press?', I answered: 'Yes, if you need it, but like everything else in golf, it can be exaggerated.' When Ben Hogan says he put his left wrist under the shaft to make an angle of 8° between the forearm and the back of the hand, he means that he found that at the time he achieved a great triumph (or triumphs), this was just the amount which worked. It may or may not be right to-day — more than

teeth and literally hit with your chin, ankles, elbows or knees — never the hands, as that is too obvious — and we know it is the catch-phrase that really gets us on to our game."

'Now this is good, sound thinking which, in closing, I would like to say is the key to the whole game. When you continue to think soundly it develops the ability to concentrate for sustained periods.'

There really is no *one* secret, unless Ben Hogan's infinite capacity for taking pains can be called a secret. The alterations players make from time to time to sections of their swings — a movement of the thumb or the foot, however small — will never work permanently: they are nothing more than temporary adjustments, almost fault-correctors. You see, it could be that, in the case of that great player Ben Hogan, his newly-found left-wrist position, where the back of the left hand, instead of being held flat in line with the left forearm, was now angled to an 8° position — the wrist was brought under the shaft — was nothing more than his insurance against a tendency to hook when under pressure.

Every player has a weakness under pressure —

Ben Hogan's newly-found left-wrist position.

14

likely he would want to alter this in some way slightly.

Once a golfer has the basic principles right and holds the club correctly, and does a smooth swing with his club, the fine adjustments have to be learned as much in competitive play as on the practice tee. There is a correct peg to hang your hat on for each day. *For a period it may be the same peg, but it is never — I repeat, never — the same peg all the time.* If a golfer plays occasional golf, such as the week-end player does, he may make a 'secret' last longer, but the hard practiser soon needs another peg for his hat.

I am certain that the inside-out theory is the soundest for the majority of golfers; to drift into a power-fade or controlled slice, as is now talked of, is a waste of time for most golfers; it means an all-round loss of length.

Golf for the big majority is an exercise and fun, and in our country there are no facilities for hitting a hundred or so balls to 'warm up', and tune-up one's swing, without the greatest inconvenience, so any method which puts the accent on the hands, and which is natural, must be right. It seems the wheel has turned and, taking a line from a popular song of the 'thirties, the latest secret is 'the oldest yet the latest thing'!

ABOVE: *Cary Middlecoff's left hand position is very sound indeed — club-face fully open.*

LEFT: *Willie Macfarlane, a U.S. Open Champion of 1925 and a great stylist. This position at the top of the back-swing taken in his heyday shows this famous player in a classical position with the club held firmly in the fingers, the left wrist well under the shaft, and the club-face fully open. This action is still worth the attention of every student and while it could be claimed that there are other positions of the wrists at this moment in the swing just as good, there are none better, and as I pen these words I cannot see the possibilities (very remote, they are) of a better one coming along.*

If any golfer can get into this position at the top of his back-swing, I cannot see how he can fail to hit good golf shots.

The first Golf Buggy ever was called a 'Linksmobile' — around 1929 it appeared, being motor-driven. Now they are mostly electric, but there are a few petrol-engine driven buggies coming in, to get rid of the battery-charging problems. This scene was in California — ideal country for such riding round, and golf is played there all the year round, too.

The first commercial sand wedge — a concave-faced job, which sold in thousands, but which was declared illegal later. This photograph is from an advertisement in a golfing magazine in 1930. It was a great club, so easy to play. I suppose it was too easy, that is why it was banned. Horton Smith brought it to Britain in 1930.

WHAT IS NEW IN GOLF AFTER ALL?

I HAVE watched the cycles of golf instruction change during the past thirty years. I have studied all the available information on golfing methods since the earliest days and I have concluded there is nothing very much new coming.

After all, what can be new? We are hitting a little white ball with a stick as far and as straight as we can, and then trying to regulate the distance and direction once the hole is within reach. There's nothing new in this.

I have watched the back-swings vary from the most upright swing to the flattest round-the-corner action possible. Yet in the hitting area *all* successful golfers arrive in a comparable position.

My picture shows the swing of James (Jimmy) Bruen from Cork, Eire, the former Amateur Champion and Walker Cup player who, as a boy prodigy in the immediate pre-war years, amazed everyone by the way he hit the ball from this super-upright back-swing. This swing is not for every golfer. Jimmy must have almost double-jointed shoulders, if such a thing is possible.

From this position he whipped the ball with an impact like the crack of a big whip and sent it enormous distances. He came on to the ball just from inside-to-out, giving it a slight hook. A ball can be hit from inside-to-out, not only from a flat back-swing but also from an upright one.

The end of the Bruen swing was classical, with the hands high.

James Bruen at the top of his back-swing (LEFT) and at the end of his swing (RIGHT).

ON BEING ORIGINAL

WHEN the courses run fast and the greens are not soaked to the extent of being puddings, then a great variety of golf shots is called for, because the ordinary pitch shot, a wedge shot if you like to push it, landing from any angle on to the putting surface, does not sit down like an egg dropped on to the pavement.

It is perhaps rather futile to tell a beginner to be original in his shots to the pin, when he is trying as hard as he can to remember what he had learned in order to hit the ball at all, but this advice to be original can be borne in mind by any golfers who consider themselves outside the beginner stage.

I know that the idea in learning golf is to groove the swing, and to simplify the game by striking every shot as nearly as possible with one swing in the same way, but the good player is always prepared to play his shot according to the occasion. It is possible, of course, to be too clever, and one sometimes meets good players who are not better ones, because they wish to complicate every shot and turn it almost into a trick one.

The beginner will ask his caddie (if he has one, that is!) how long the shot is, and then take the appropriate club and hit the shot, missing through lack of experience a few details concerning the lie, the wind or the nature of the ground and the putting surface to which he is playing — things that a more experienced player would notice.

I wonder if many of you realize what passes through the mind of a first-class player when he is playing, say, a pitch to the green. Before he plays the shot he has decided many points. For example, he has decided that for the lie in question and the certain type of green being approached, it is better to play a full No. 8 than a half No. 7, as he can get more grip on the ball.

He has noticed the wind; if he is not quite sure of the direction he has found out with a handkerchief held high or by throwing up some little bits of grass. He has observed, too, which side of the green the pin is placed, so if there is any serious trouble near the pin, he can play safe, if the occasion demands, and a risk must not be taken.

Serious trouble such as a bad bunker, a clump of gorse, a pond or some long grass or even an out of bounds fence, are all looked for. So, before he plays his shot, he has weighed up all these points, for it is one of the conditions of being a first-class player to think first and not afterwards.

It might be interesting for some of you who travel around and play on different courses to ask yourselves after your first round what you remember of the course, apart from the approximate length of the holes and the scratch score. I am certain many golfers have a job to remember where the serious trouble lies on every hole, unless they have visited it and been punished.

As an old competition player, I found myself looking for all the two-stroke penalties automatically — the out of bounds boundaries and the places where a ball could be lost. One-stroke penalties, although severe, seem to impress one less, but long grass near the green or deep straight-sided bunkers must be avoided at all costs.

Let us return to the question of being original with those little shots around the green. One of the

An interesting study of the 'Old Maestro' James Braid playing a pitch and run shot. This famous old champion, living most of his life on fast-running Walton Heath, where there are few built-up greens — most of the greens run straight off the fairway and so are on the same level — used this shot as one of the main features of his armoury.

In this stroke he has made *the ball run. The whole angle of the body and weight situation show that he has been ahead of the ball all the time, so as to play it down, but has used his hands to push the club-head to the hole, allowing the club-face to turn over very slightly. This is really playing the shot naturally.*

Note the white linen jacket — a relic of the days when pullovers had not yet come into fashion.

17

ABOVE: *English Amateur Golf Championship at the Royal Cinque Ports Golf Club, Deal, Kent. H. G. Bentley is approaching the 13th green. He has gone right down the grip and has used his club-face as the extension of his right hand. He was an ace at making-up shots. Anthony Spalding, who wrote the golf articles in the London* Star *for many years, is the hatless spectator.*

RIGHT: *These shots are not stunts — but actual efficient, legal golf strokes, and the only real way to get a good result from such lies. In the drawing (page 19) taken from an actual photograph, the golfer broke his club (1) but he could have got the same result standing in the position seen in drawing (2).*

I am seen demonstrating a shot backwards and through the legs, made necessary because of the lie by the tree. The other shot was necessary, because the bunker, just through the gap at St Andrews on the 13th hole, is so deep that even if I had stood in it I still could not play the ball. I could hardly see it from the sand. I had no room to stand if I stood normally to the ball, but this way I knocked it forward a few yards. A left-hander, of course, could have played this shot readily, but I could not guarantee a successful shot at all with a right-handed club held nose downwards, especially from a poor lie. To-day few people carry a left-handed club; luckily such situations are rare, but this is a way to meet one.

hardest is the shot played against the grain of the grass, from the walk to the next tee for example. Here the club buries itself on the down-and-through action and the ball never seems to get into the air properly. There is no doubt that a tight grip of the club is essential, and that an action whereby the follow-through is 'lifted', the opposite of the chop type of stroke, is best. These shots are a guess anyway. I have tried them with straighter-faced clubs, too, but that is not the answer, though

it might work for some shots, where loft is not needed on the ball, because there is less tendency to dig for the ball.

Pitch and run shots are the shots which seem to have gone out of fashion since the wedge came into modern golf, yet they are the real safety ones for the handicap golfer. I have one golfing friend who still uses one of those special short-shafted, square-handled run-up clubs which were popular not long ago; now they are rarely to be seen. This

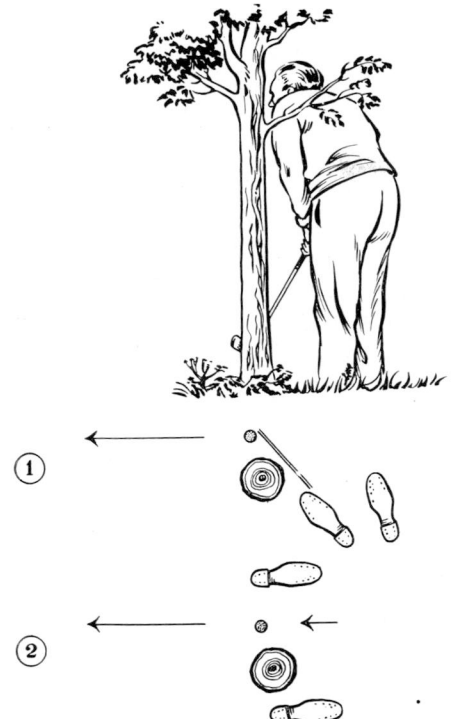

Playing from behind a tree (see page 18).

day, has been Harry Bradshaw, and he overlaps two or three fingers.

James Braid, living so long on fast-running Walton Heath, with scarcely any built-up greens, was a great player of original strokes, and these were very wristy affairs, often accompanied by a kick through with the right knee and a pronounced rolling over of the club-face as if to make sure the ball was to roll. He made a run-up shot look like one in the way he played it.

In the category of original shots would come the chop shot when a ball lying poorly cannot safely be 'got at' with the standard stroke. I often feel that this shot is justified if there is a danger of 'hitting one thin' or of being timid about forcing the ball up a slope as on a double plateau green, because this stroke, which of necessity has a definite attack on the ball, gives less time for a change of mind, as often happens during the normal stroke, if the player has any doubts about the power required. Naturally only when the ground is firm can this sort of shot be a great success. I know some middle handicap range players who rely on the chop to win their half-crowns! To stab at the ball, as often occurs in this sort of shot,

was the only club in his bag he really knew. He scuffled the ball along with the minimum of pitch on it, and through experience often gauged the fairway and semi-rough a treat. There used to be a club called a 'scuffler', which like other clubs such as the jigger and lofting iron has also had its day.

Since top golfers began to use their body action in a pronounced way on the shorter shots, original shots have fallen out of the repertoire of many good golfers. They do not seek to play them, they 'play round' them.

Few handicap golfers notice when sand bunkers have no lips on them, and so often miss a chance to roll the ball out of trouble; and if the ball has to be rolled, then always use a putter — a straight-faced iron does not give the same result.

If you are in front of a big green and need to produce a shot which you could do best if you could lob it by hand, underarm, do not overlook the fact that if you overlap two fingers of the right hand on the left, the right shoulder comes up a fraction and it becomes easier to flip the ball forward cleanly. A divot is not required for such shots, and remember that possibly the best pitch and runner in the business, since Bobby Jones's

ABOVE: *Single-figure handicap, experienced American golfer, Mr Paul Summers, from Lewisburg, W. Virginia, plays a difficult shot from the top of this bunker. The feature of this successful shot, which incidentally went to the hole side, is the body balance and the long back swing. There is a tendency from such positions to swing too quickly and snatch at the shot. There is no doubt that Mr Summers trusted his swing here and 'waited for it'.*

19

is by no means a classical stroke, but it should not be overlooked by those who are inclined to come up too readily on the shorter shots to the pin, even if it is only used to learn to strike the ball definitely.

With the old-fashioned thin-soled niblick, with a sharpish cutting edge, the modern skid through blast from the sand was 'never on', and so the leading golfers learned to shock the ball from the sand, by actually burying the head behind the ball, varying distances, and shocking the ball on the green by the force of the explosion. This explosion shot to-day is almost out of date, but if the ball lies badly in soft sand, it *is* often easiest to lay open the face of the narrow-soled No. 9 iron and explode the ball, following the old-fashioned method. The broad-soled wedge or sand iron with the lower back edge to the sole, made for skidding, is more difficult to handle if the lie of the ball is bad and, being heavy, is more difficult to swing fast at the ball. The sand iron is made for skidding slowly, not for exploding.

So many golfers would benefit from playing rounds with only five clubs — and I do not mean only club golfers; I include the top players, too — because it is the only way to learn to play golf. It is possible, and fable has it that it did happen, for a golfer to go straight from a driving range complete with sand bunker and putting green, where he had trained, to win an open competition. He would be playing on soft watered greens and on a course with no rough, but just set him off for the first time on a real seaside links, or the Walton

This is one of the hardest shots to judge in the whole game — playing the ball from a ditch. The only way to succeed in such a stroke, if you must take the risk of playing it, is to keep very still with the body and rely on your hands to lead the clubhead to the ball — doing the minimum of arm swing. Marcel Chassagny of Paris in action.

Heath courses, where originality pays off, and he could never have acquired enough experience to handle the problems which arise in every round. I did not hear how he got a handicap, if he had one worse than scratch!

ANALYSING YOUR OWN MISTAKES

THE average golfer, who can be counted upon to mishit the ball more times in a round than not, never tries even to analyse his faults. He never stops to work out, from the unsatisfactory flight of the ball he has produced, why it happened.

Its direction and trajectory should be studied — there is always an explanation. Take, as an example for study, a ball that starts off flying low to the left and then rises quickly, curves to the right, and on landing breaks to the right and stops — a sort of pulled slice. Or consider the ball which starts off to the right, then curves to the left, ducks downward, and then scuttles along the ground as if it would never stop — the quick hook.

The first thing to do is to study the mechanics of the golf swing, to figure out which fundamental or fundamentals must have been violated, then find a trick or a tip which will serve to prevent a repetition of the violation. In the first example, the clubhead is obviously coming across the ball from outside to inside, and the hit is made particularly late with the club-face striking a glancing blow as well, accompanied by a determined effort with the hands to hold the club-face down. This outside-in attack, plus the glancing blow, produces a very fast spinning ball which, once the initial pull flight, due to the swing being out of line, is beaten by the power of the spin, curves away to the right.

The cause of this type of error? Insufficient body pivot in the back-swing fails to bring the club-shaft pointing parallel to the line from the ball to the hole (some players, Locke and O'Connor, for example, point not just to the hole, but far to the right of it, as viewed from behind), so from this position the club descends all too easily on the inside of the line of play and then has to travel on the inside-to-out path to strike the ball at all.

It can also happen that the player, even if getting into the correct position at the top of the swing, begins to unwind his shoulders too early; that is, before the arms have had a chance to drag the hands and the club into the correct groove.

Also, if too much right shoulder is applied, the wrists will not have enough time to get the club-head through to strike the ball a square blow; it will be from outside-in again, with the club-face generally open at impact. To cure this fault, the player must learn to attack the ball on an inside-to-out path, and so it is a good idea to set up a simple sort of control for acquiring this movement, such as I have set out.

Draw a line on a bare piece of ground with a peg tee, using a club-shaft as a guide, and tee up low or place on the ground a golf ball in the centre of the line. Place long peg tees in the ground as indicated in the sketch. It should be possible to strike the ball without touching the tees; and if the hands are bringing the clubhead through correctly and in time, there should be a good result. Make sure that the left arm is in charge and that the clubhead is being swung straight on. The shoulders must move under the head and not around it, so that the clubhead can get on the inside-to-out path. If the peg tees, which must be tall ones, are touched during the swing, then the player can see for himself where his error lies. It is important in this action that the hands do not get too far ahead of the ball as impact approaches.

In the second example the line of attack of the clubhead is on an excessive inside-to-out path,

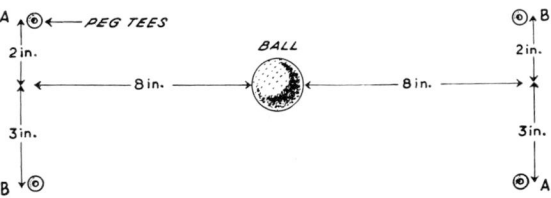

with the toe of the face of the club making contact with the ball first and with the hit being early as well. This is just about as much the opposite of the first example as is possible, for slices and hooks are in pairs, so the very points which are down to be cured in the first example can be accentuated in the second. By this I mean that a swing at the ball from inside-to-out, as in the drawing from A to A, can send the ball out to the right, as a push, if the face is square to the line hit, or if the face is square 'line to hole', then the ball will have a hook on it. Thus a push and a hook are a pair; they come from the same angle of attack on the ball.

Conversely the slice and pull are a pair for the

It is difficult to slice the ball from here. Christy O'Connor points the clubhead to the right of the hole. Note how he relaxes the left hand. This is not suitable for everyone, but it relieves tension and if the club-shaft does not turn all can be well.

same reason that the clubhead travels on line B to B. It is important to know all this.

To cure a quick hook

An effort must be made to take the clubhead forward (towards the tee box, that is); a shoulder turn can be used, the right side can be rolled round to throw the club towards an outside-to-in path, and the left arm drag-down can be accentuated to produce a later hit, which will tend to hold the club-face more open as impact approaches, to stop the toe of the club-face from leading up to the ball first.

Part of the cause of this second error can come from the grip itself. The placing of the hands on the shaft has a very big bearing on the angle of the swing and on the wrist action itself, and one slight alteration may often call for other adjustments which must be done to get any benefit.

To help to develop a hook, see that the left hand does not show *more* than two knuckles and that the backs of the hands are parallel.

To help to cure a hook, see that the thumb of the right hand is on top of the shaft and that the right hand is being used to guide the club-face.

These tips are my own, but I have found, despite their apparent contradiction to the accepted doctrines, they are 100% right.

THE NATURAL GOLFER

Is there such a person? It has always been admitted by players who have never taken a lesson, and who play well, that they have copied from other players, stealing something here and there as they develop their own style. This means that, honestly speaking, they have a sort of composite style which masquerades under the name of 'The Natural Golfer'. Yet, all the same, I did come across a golfer who had never taken a lesson, and who had not copied anyone.

A strong young fellow he was, rather stocky and with thick short-fingered hands, who had gone round a golf course more or less regularly for ten years, slogging at his game on the course and never practising. After reaching some sort of peak to his game — in which a pitch shot always meant a try to scoop the ball in the air and where 'one off the sole' which skidded along the ground caused him to comment naturally, 'I didn't get under that one' — his whole game had fallen to pieces. There

was nothing one could do to help.

Even the standard expressions 'look at the ball', 'swing slower', 'take your time', etc., had no helping effect; in fact, at one moment I felt that any suggestion I made was making the worst quite horrible. The picture of the 'Natural Golfer' — I regret I did not photograph him — was like this: a narrow stance, hands somewhat apart, with right hand well underneath, ball well outside the left toe, and the general aim to mid-on, anticipating a slice; but it was 'even money' that the catching hold of the club again on the way down, as the shaft turned during the back swing, brought the face of the club often very closed to the ball, and this meant a smother or a pulled ball as often as a slice, which of course happened when the face of the club arrived square at impact.

'I have done jolly well my own way until recently', said the 'Natural Golfer', 'but now it has all gone. I am afraid to take any lessons in case I go worse.' 'Sir', I had to reply, 'there is no way to go worse except to miss the ball altogether.'

The swing, I forgot to mention, consisted of a short, waist-high action with a lot of 'ballet' footwork accompanied by a shoulder roll, as it were, just to make it more difficult.

We managed to fit in four lessons, in which some of the mysteries were unfolded, but during the round where we met I managed to get the 'Natural Golfer' stabbing successfully at his wedge shots, and so hitting the ball downwards, to make it rise, and not expecting it to come upwards with a scooping action. This was the best I could get while playing on the course. To learn to swing inside-to-out, to use the hands correctly, to pivot sufficiently, to swing back to the horizontal, to hold on to the club, to follow through towards the hole, to keep the head steady — these made a fine collection of things to do, or to attempt to do.

Progress was made, and I thought that the swing finally achieved did look like a golf swing, but it could not be claimed as precise. What was gained definitely was that when I asked the 'Natural Golfer' to show me what his old swing looked like, he had already forgotten it enough to be against trying to reproduce it.

I suppose what really is meant by a natural golfer is 'one who makes the game look easy' in a natural sort of way. Just two extremes flash to mind — a natural player making the game look easy — Percy Alliss (senior); and one making it look difficult — Max Faulkner, when he has no need to do so.

Harry Bradshaw, who overlaps two or three fingers of his right hand on his left, is a natural player all right. Not for him any thoughts of straight left arm, unwinding of the hips first, etc. This sturdy Irishman has as his programme 'A ball is there! I must hit it straight and hard.' He thinks of nothing else.

The Duke of Norfolk is a natural golfer and is an above-average player, for the time he can give the game.
LEFT: *A good left-hand grip, but a palm grip with the right hand.* CENTRE: *The club slips into the fingers quite naturally coming through.* RIGHT: *A classical putting stroke with an old-time wooden putter.*

Monsignor Hugh O'Flaherty and Father John Murray, S.J., at the Rome Golf Club.

LEFT: *Monsignor Hugh O'Flaherty of Rome, the 'Scarlet Pimpernel of the Vatican', who helped so many allied prisoners to safety during the last war, loves his game of golf. He plays to a 5 handicap with this 'natural' grip of the club. A natural golfer if ever there was one!* CENTRE: *Horace G. Hutchinson, Amateur Champion in 1886–7. This is how a golfer played at the turn of the century. Note bent left arm, bent right leg action, Norfolk Jacket and palm grip and open right hand.* RIGHT: *This was the back-swing of a legendary hero, Lt. F. G. Tait, killed in the Boer War as a young man. Note here the left hand position and the grip of the right hand. This is certainly a natural action!*

CURING THE TWITCH

'TWITCHING' on the short shots, from the little holing-out putts up to the 30-yard pitch or pitch and run, is not perhaps the most common fault of the average golfer, but once I was a bit shaken to come across two such 'sufferers' in one week. One 19 handicap and the other 9, both 'crazy' golfers being driven almost crazy by this appalling disease. Even from the front of an open green, with just a well-cut apron before them and a No. 6 iron in their hands, the clubhead could not be brought to the ball except in a jerk — a jerk in which the club either hit the ball very cleanly or caught the ground behind the ball suddenly!

One of these golfers told me the tale, very sadly, of how he was given up by his pro., whom he had taken out one evening in the summer to get him to help him. After trying out many ideas, the pro. had taken a club to show him how to play the stroke, and after finding himself twitching on three successive shots, had decided to leave him before he, too, became permanently affected. Rather cowardly, I thought! This may or may not be exactly true, but there are many golfers who believe that such twitching is entirely mental and a job for the psychiatrist.

I believe that it can develop from a doubt about

Charles Ward tries the reverse hands style for putting, to get rid of the 'over 40 twitch'. He uses this as a temporary cure, then goes back to his old style.

being able to play such a shot smoothly in the first place, and that successive failures can bring this twitch about; but there is also a fundamental error in technique.

In the case of the player who nearly gave it to his pro., on closer observation, when I asked him to grip a near-by umbrella, I could see he was always going to have trouble from holding the club in the way he did — his right hand was not well placed; it was in a curious bunched-up position and so much under the shaft that a real wrist cock with this hand seemed unlikely.

I said I would look at his action on the first occasion and, following a 'phone call, he came round to show me 'the real thing' in my garden, where it is possible to pitch into a net from ten to twelve yards.

Yes! there it was, alive, a real twitch. It was repeated consistently, accompanied by a change in complexion, for as the terror grew his face became more red, not entirely from shame, for we were alone, but from the effort of concentrating and the job of trying to make the clubhead swing. It did not swing, it was taken back from the ball a short distance and then suddenly it tried to fly at the ball, like a dog at a rat. In a dozen attempts, a 'mixed bag' was offered, including 'one off the pipe' which hit some stone steps on the right, whence the ball popped back into the garden pond.

What should one do? I am always sure a cure can be effected, because there is a physical reason for such mistakes. 'Chop down on it. Do not follow through, get the hands ahead of the shaft and then squeeze the ball into the mat! Pinch it!'

No! this did not help much, for there was not enough golfing ability in the player to get this idea quickly enough, and I did not intend, therefore, to plug this suggestion.

'Now get your hands lower at the address', I suggested. Yes, this was a bit better, a series of quite satisfying shots pitched down the paving-stones of the yard correctly and bounced into the net. But after another dozen shots or so, the old twitch showed up again. That was not it!

A change of stance was helpful, but with the right foot wanting all the time to point outwards like paraded feet, toes out 45°, it was not easy to move the right hip and knee with the stroke.

Here it was — not in the grip or hand-work really, but as much in the feet as the hips. The right side locked, and the shoulders did not move freely, as there was no rhythm in the action — there never could be.

'Oh, I keep my head still. I never look up', the golfer said, and that was true; he had added a 'head-frozen-into-position' section to this already paralysed motion.

How did he ever get on to the green at all? For I could see it would sometimes need a chain of these strokes to advance twenty yards? Well, he finally took a putter and with this 22-ounce club he could record every time a success, for he always made a contact with the ball and so got on to the putting surface. It was just that one shot, from in front of the green, which 'killed him'. I could not get him to stay put with his feet parallel — his right foot always wanted to turn out — but by not getting the weight on the heels, and by using the inside edges of the shoes, the body began to come 'into' the swing of the clubhead.

What sort of an eye had he got? Yes, he had played all the games at school, and decently, too! Let me check on that. 'Here are five balls on the mat! Just knock them into the net without addressing the ball and without a pause of any sort.' BANG, BANG, BANG, BANG and BANG — the whole lot flew immediately to the centre of the net.

Joe Davis, the billiards and snooker ace, tries out his hand for steadiness at the 'News of the World' Garden Party in the Chairman's garden. The idea is to pass the wire loop he is holding along the electrified line without touching it. A bell rings if contact is made and the distance covered is measured, a prize being given if you get to the end. This is not difficult to do if you have good sight, I found. As the years pass, it is difficult for the eyes to hold the focus on the loop in the wire, to judge exactly 'where it is'. Joe, a keen golfer, is just a sound putter, not a master on the greens as one might expect. His handicap at his pet game, snooker, to-day is just 'scratch' in golf terms, he reckons. Anno domini and eyesight problems have put up his handicap, for he was plus 10 for years. Unbeatable that means — and he was for twenty years.

Sam Snead practising putting at Boca Raton — beyond, his golf buggy waits for him to begin a round. He is trying out my old putter and his left hand action holding the blade down is interesting, but on short putts this closed face action can provoke pushing out the ball to the right.

As I thought, he could produce a result if he could get the club back from the ball.

'Now play me some shots with no wrist work. Swing from the shoulders, point the left shoulder towards the ball and without help from the wrists swing the clubhead under your head, allowing the knees and hips to work — a sort of wooden doll action!' This was it — it worked like magic, shot after shot went sweetly into the centre of the net. But the ball was perched up nicely on the bristles of the mat, quite teed up in fact.

Sam Snead, one of the greatest golfers ever, snapped without his straw hat on this occasion, suffered for a while from a twitch in his short putts. On a long putt, as shown here, he is perhaps the equal of anybody in the game. This photograph shows the follow-through on a 30-foot putt at Boca Raton, Florida, where he goes in the winter.

the flag in the centre of the fairway. They anticipated another easy win. He never came back, so I trust it *is* all over. A doctor friend of mine claims to have satisfied himself that 'jitters' and 'putting paralysis' come from concentrating on the clubhead instead of the hands only. He claims that the hands form the most sensitive part of the golfer's body, for in them are placed highly sensitive sensory organs which can give the golfer the most vital information.

No golfer twitches when he moves his hands backwards and forwards as when making a golf stroke, if he has no club in his hands. I have checked this point with various golfers. To ask a not very skilful golfer to watch his hands move and not to have his eye on the ball might prove to be a mixed blessing, but there is something in it.

Charles Ward, as can be seen in the photograph on page 24, is using a reverse hands grip of the club to get rid of a twitch. I have seen low handicap golfers and professionals, too, even putt left-handed to get the missing rhythm back and to cut out that jerk.

If I were setting out to cure all twitches, I would not consult a psychiatrist but a physician, and get my metabolism fixed up. I think the nerves need feeding; just my humble opinion!

Would it work off the fairway? Yes, if the lie was good. Winter rules, anyway, I told him, would see him through for the present. I do not guarantee that this suggestion will prove to be the permanent cure, but it did seem as if it would break the spell.

This player was afraid to move away from the ball because he felt that to take the clubhead back more than nine or ten inches was risking an inaccurate blow, yet he was soon satisfied that he could 'find the ball' easily, even 'on the run'.

I did not mention the right-hand position again after I moved the right thumb from a sort of floating position so that it was right down the top of the shaft.

I do not know if there is to be a 'happy ever after ending', but my golfer was going to test it out the very next week-end on his regular 'clients'. He hoped to stop them rubbing their hands together with glee when they saw his good second shots finish just that right number of yards from

Another get-rid-of-twitch method. This is perhaps the most popular of all. Charles Mills in action. Several well-known amateurs, including Leonard Crawley and John Beck, are putting croquet-fashion.

GOOD GOLF WITHOUT PRACTICE?

To the European golf fan, unless he has visited America, it is difficult to imagine what goes on in the golf world there, for there is an enthusiasm for the game which cannot be described — it must be seen. Down in Florida, where golf courses are being built by the dozen, as this all-the-year-round holiday State grows in popularity annually, golf course construction design incorporates facilities for practice which I have never yet seen in Europe, except in the American military courses in Germany. Even at a long-established club like the elegant Gulf Stream Golf Club, where Bobby Cruikshank has been pro. for some twenty years, one finds two huge putting greens, a small pitching green and practice bunker, and a driving range where a pail of one hundred balls costs two dollars. The interest in reading about the game was never greater, and short golf articles by Tommy Armour, Cary Middlecoff and Sam Snead appear in many daily papers, often illustrated by drawings, year after year.

Ben Hogan had a similar series running for some time. He wrote also a long article for *Life*, in which he gave *the secret* of his success — for just ten thousand dollars — built around the permitting of his left wrist to go a little more under the shaft at the top of the back swing, and for the forearm and back of the hand not to be in line, as he had recommended at one time.

In the elaborate series (about 8,000 words in each article), which was beautifully illustrated with coloured drawings (now published in book form), Ben wrote of his own action in the greatest detail, developing all his ideas most carefully. No golfer can fail to be interested in how this golfing wizard plays, for even nearing fifty years of age he is still one of the world's top players. He practises with a determination few youngsters show. I enjoyed following this series because they set out so clearly all the points Hogan studies when he plays and practises, but, of course, they must be read with the understanding that the writer is very strong and wiry, and has *exceptionally* strong hands.

If you would give me a would-be golfer with hands as strong as any top professional's, then three-quarters of the problems of learning to play golf are solved. Most golfers fail because they have *no hands*, not because they do a bad swing. All the efforts they make to swing the club at the ball are finally transmitted by the hands, and if the hands are weak, then the back-swing, however good, all too frequently leads to nothing, because there is no control of the club in the hitting area.

Gulf Stream Golf Club. One of the putting greens in front of the clubhouse. Florida, 1957.

Peter Mills, one of our best professionals, is not considered a good practiser by his colleagues here — he prefers to play. My camera has caught him practising in Spain at the Barcelona Golf Club, 1957. His action is classical. I like the firm left hand and the club-face position.

While studying the Hogan series for the first time it struck me that the author had accepted too readily that those he had set out to guide have strong hands and muscular bodies, because he

THE GOLF SECRET

THIS is the title of a golf book by a West Country doctor, Dr H. A. Murray.

Golf books and articles are poured out by the thousand, it seems, for there is no other sport in the world which is submitted to such an annual barrage of words the year round, the world over.

Dr Murray has done what so many other instructional writers on golf do: he has selected one section of the golf swing and developed his theme to the point of 'proving it a secret'. There is a lot of sound sense in this book, and it is a great credit to the writer. Winding up his work, the Doctor says: 'Apart from maintaining a firm grip, there are only four anatomical parts with which we are consciously concerned in executing the golf swing. They are the upper part of the spine, the left shoulder and the left and right upper arms. The first is used in preparation for the swing, the third and fourth can be left to themselves; the second is indispensable. Therefore, the LEFT SHOULDER is our sheet-anchor.'

I still have to be convinced that golf, for the world in general, means using more body than I teach, for I give the body only 15% of the effort to get speed, the arms, hands and wrists 85%. (Seymour Dunn, a great teacher and student, gave the same percentages).

When one teaches golf to dozens of different people of all ages, shapes and sizes, it becomes increasingly clear that each one is an individual case. There are fundamentals, maybe, that one can follow, but it is always a question of using one's experience of trial and error methods to save the pupil from wasting his or her time, attempting to do the impossible. And yet at the outset every pupil imagines he or she will develop that perfect 'pro. swing'.

Just as further evidence of the need to be original when teaching — a very broad-shouldered person, who cannot get his elbows anywhere near touching when his arms are extended before him, cannot possibly hit the ball with that ideal sort of flapping action of the right hand, because his right hand will lie too much under the shaft at the address, so he will need to use a pushing action, or even a 'hand slide' by the club shaft to get his best results.

I am often amused by golfers who are afraid to go to a certain professional because they feel they cannot 'do' his method. They might as well say: 'We have not your power or flexibility, therefore we could not adopt your method.'

This would imply that the pro. only gets pupils to teach who can or do use his method. How wrong! I do think that a *stiff-armed, body emphasized swing* is no good for the average golfer, who is a person past the dashing activity of youth; it is, in fact, a spine-twisting menace. A pivot is essential — it goes along with the swing — but I hesitate to make my pupils do a pivot forcibly or to insist on the body winding and unwinding any more than will happen with the steady to-and-fro swinging of a heavy club.

The instructor who has long experience usually tries out his stock phrases and methods on every beginner, and is then prepared to adjust, because every person requires a different approach. To perhaps three people in six, a simple sort of accepted explanation fails to ring the bell; another phrase, maybe, has to be tried to put over the idea — perhaps several attempts are needed. Because of this, I always view with suspicion a method which says 'this is it'. Do you remember the much vaunted 'scissor' action — the crossing over of the wrists? The secret of the game, it was said to be. It is forgotten to-day, considered almost as out-of-date as the hickory shaft, *yet* it could be the right medicine for some players to-day who are afraid to let the wrists go free.

Treat your left shoulder as a key pivot of the swing. It points to the ball 'going up', and then it revolves around and under the head till it is pulled behind the head as the swing proceeds, the right shoulder taking its place momentarily; but would it count for you as '*the* secret'?

It could possibly be the very thing you need to accentuate, but, like other tips, it can be overdone and so exceed its real rôle. There are several types of golf swing and, I am sure, they will one day be set out in the form of a chart. Swing one — this will be a certain grip, and certain body and foot actions to go with it; variations for certain builds and degrees of flexibility. So a player could find his swing and then add all the bits that fit together for him as parts for his own jigsaw puzzle. That will be the day! Swing two — this will be a different grip and its accompanying variations of body and foot action, but it will then be understood that parts of swing one and swing two are not interchangeable. So many mistakes are made by keen golfers in copying swings or bits of swings and adding them to their own actions, which they just won't fit.

WHAT SHAPE ARE YOU?

EVERYONE is built differently physically. And from this simple statement comes the great truth, that it is no use trying to imitate another player in every detail — it does not work out.

It was interesting to read some words of Bill Campbell's, captain of the 1955 U.S. Walker Cup team which butchered our players at St Andrews, in which he was acknowledging his deep admiration for golfer Sam Snead and at the same time pointing out that Sam's powerful double-jointed, much broken and repaired bones in his hands give him a unique grip of the club.

His long arms and loose shoulders enable him to develop as wide an arc at impact as can be found in the whole game. Most golfers would love to have, as one golfer imaginatively said in a New Year's wish, a swing like Slamming Sam's, 'just for a couple of days, then I'd show the boys!'

I have watched over the years the champions of yester-year having to alter their actions to fit their changing bodies, as with the fleeting years their legs have got weaker and bodies thicker. Ben Hogan decided to free himself gradually from the dreadful strain of big golf and its preparation; he put on 20 lb. and went to around 12 stone in weight. This alone made him alter his body action and made his hands and arms play an ever bigger rôle.

The tall thin players have completely different problems from thick-set, short types, and I have seen that the thick-set players, when they have put

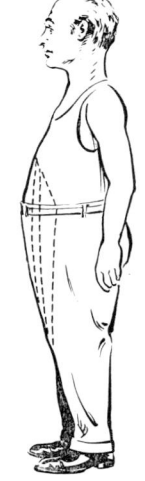

What's my line? Don't kid yourself! It really does make a difference, if you want to copy someone, just to see where your line runs.

on weight, rely very much on an opening and closing of the hands during the swing in order to play a decent game at all — and then their play would only be a patch on their best, younger days.

When one knows this, and when one sees a fifty-year-old beginner struggling to do a swing which a pro. with almost forty years of contact with the game could not reproduce, one realises that the golf game must always be approached with a very open mind. To be prepared to try everything and anything should be every golfer's plan, because every golfer can improve up to the limit of his own capabilities. Few senior golfers, even the very keenest ones, are disposed to try and develop muscles or loosen up tight ones with exercises and massage. They rightly regard golf as a game, but this does not get them away from the fact that golf muscles are needed to do a golfing swing. Ask your own professional (or several professionals) what he thinks your peak would be in golf, according to the amount of practice and play you can manage, and this will give you a goal. If you get there, then obviously you will raise your sights.

I have always stuck to my theories about the right physique for golf, because golf is more difficult for extremes; very tall or very short people have entirely different problems to handle. Gene Sazaren, one of the best little (in size) golfers of the past three decades, had to use a considerable body sway going up to get his back-swing arc wide enough, because with his shorter radius, left shoulder-joint to clubhead, he naturally had too narrow or steep an arc for wooden shots, if he stayed still on the back-swing.

Fred Daly uses his most personal shoulder roll-away from the ball to get width in his back-swing

Marcel Dallemagne of Paris, tall and slim.

c

Archie Compsto[n]

because he too is a sho
(Archie Compston, I
Barnes, Bernard Hu
mind) have the oppo
left shoulder to clubh
be narrowed for most
ston uses a very delay
as possible, with a bo
way down.

Tall (Open Champ
Middlecoff sway noti
have to, because a sm
the ground can only b
range of arcs. An arc
ground behind the bal
the ball too much. Th
matters slightly, as th
ball is 0·84 inches off
0·81 inches with the si
makes a mighty differ
spongy turf the larger
ground-level, and it is
the ball more 'coming

The players of idea
Hogan, Locke, Nelson
include myself for bei
fewer problems of the
wide arc is just right to
the tee and through the

The smaller player
short-game players, for
are very convenient for

There must be a difference in the swings of these two golfers. Mario Gonzales from Brazil, 'the Walking Pencil' as he was called in 1948, had a hip action which could be called snake-like. He used it to get power and to hold the club-face open, as his grip was part of the beginning of a shut-faced club action.

Harry Lipman, of the sturdy figure, has the opposite problems — the problems of the short golfer with the extra weight on; his objective is to move more, not less, and to try to get some hip action into his swing to stop the shoulders doing too much. He should never stand still at the address, his feet should be 'alive', he should begin his swing back from a 'little dance'.

LEFT: *Double-jointed James Adams, pro. at Royal Mid-Surrey Golf Club, can do the most rhythmic full swing even with both feet flat on the ground. Although now a veteran he can still swing as fully and as smoothly as he ever did.*

CENTRE: *Thick-set, short, sturdy Lionel Hebert, U.S. Ryder Cup player, a successful player on the Tournament Circuit, stands very near to the ball for his short shots. He is really 'crowding the ball'. I find this is a personal position — it looks cramped to me. Many would shank the ball from here.*

RIGHT: *The shoulders here work horizontally instead of under the head — the head has moved far to the right, throwing the whole swing off balance, and the bent right leg stops the swing from ever being firm. This closed club-face position and crumpled-up backswing make it difficult to stay on the 'inside of the ball'. This golfer does not use his height, and the ball is generally cut miserably. The real golf muscles are missing — that is why this happens.*

34

WHAT SHAPE ARE YOU?

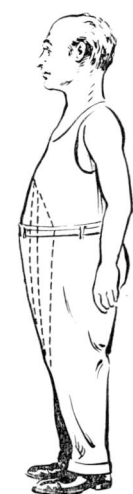

EVERYONE is built differently physically. And from this simple statement comes the great truth, that it is no use trying to imitate another player in every detail — it does not work out.

It was interesting to read some words of Bill Campbell's, captain of the 1955 U.S. Walker Cup team which butchered our players at St Andrews, in which he was acknowledging his deep admiration for golfer Sam Snead and at the same time pointing out that Sam's powerful double-jointed, much broken and repaired bones in his hands give him a unique grip of the club.

His long arms and loose shoulders enable him to develop as wide an arc at impact as can be found in the whole game. Most golfers would love to have, as one golfer imaginatively said in a New Year's wish, a swing like Slamming Sam's, 'just for a couple of days, then I'd show the boys!'

I have watched over the years the champions of yester-year having to alter their actions to fit their changing bodies, as with the fleeting years their legs have got weaker and bodies thicker. Ben Hogan decided to free himself gradually from the dreadful strain of big golf and its preparation; he put on 20 lb. and went to around 12 stone in weight. This alone made him alter his body action and made his hands and arms play an ever bigger rôle.

The tall thin players have completely different problems from thick-set, short types, and I have seen that the thick-set players, when they have put

What's my line? Don't kid yourself! It really does make a difference, if you want to copy someone, just to see where your line runs.

on weight, rely very much on an opening and closing of the hands during the swing in order to play a decent game at all — and then their play would only be a patch on their best, younger days.

When one knows this, and when one sees a fifty-year-old beginner struggling to do a swing which a pro. with almost forty years of contact with the game could not reproduce, one realises that the golf game must always be approached with a very open mind. To be prepared to try everything and anything should be every golfer's plan, because every golfer can improve up to the limit of his own capabilities. Few senior golfers, even the very keenest ones, are disposed to try and develop muscles or loosen up tight ones with exercises and massage. They rightly regard golf as a game, but this does not get them away from the fact that golf muscles are needed to do a golfing swing. Ask your own professional (or several professionals) what he thinks your peak would be in golf, according to the amount of practice and play you can manage, and this will give you a goal. If you get there, then obviously you will raise your sights.

I have always stuck to my theories about the right physique for golf, because golf is more difficult for extremes; very tall or very short people have entirely different problems to handle. Gene Sazaren, one of the best little (in size) golfers of the past three decades, had to use a considerable body sway going up to get his back-swing arc wide enough, because with his shorter radius, left shoulder-joint to clubhead, he naturally had too narrow or steep an arc for wooden shots, if he stayed still on the back-swing.

Fred Daly uses his most personal shoulder roll-away from the ball to get width in his back-swing

Marcel Dallemagne of Paris, tall and slim.

31

Archie Compston   *Byron Nelson*   *Eric Brown*

because he too is a short man. The very tall players (Archie Compston, David Thomas, 'Long Jim' Barnes, Bernard Hunt, Peter Alliss, come to mind) have the opposite problem; their radius, left shoulder to clubhead, is large, and so has to be narrowed for most fairway shots, and Compston uses a very delayed hit and as narrow an arc as possible, with a body sway into the ball on the way down.

Tall (Open Champions) Jim Barnes and Cary Middlecoff sway noticeably into the ball. They have to, because a small golf ball when lying on the ground can only be attacked within a limited range of arcs. An arc can be too wide and hit the ground behind the ball, or too steep and squeeze the ball too much. The larger-sized ball does ease matters slightly, as the centre of the back of the ball is 0·84 inches off bare ground level as against 0·81 inches with the small ball; and this little bit makes a mighty difference, because allowing for spongy turf the larger balls sit up higher off bare ground-level, and it is, therefore, possible to hit the ball more 'coming up'.

The players of ideal average physique (Snead, Hogan, Locke, Nelson and myself — I immodestly include myself for being of similar height) have fewer problems of the arc to solve — our natural wide arc is just right to hit the ball in the back off the tee and through the green.

The smaller players usually become expert short-game players, for their natural steepish arcs are very convenient for the shorter-shafted pitch-

ing clubs, with which the ball has always to be hit a descending blow. Peter Thomson is a slightly stiffer edition of the immortal Bobby Jones. Jones was not considered a great pitcher, but that was just because he played his shots to the pin with the same lazy rhythm which he used for his long shots. I am not positive, but I feel I am correct in blaming his training with hickory shafts as being responsible

Peter Thomson, a stockier Bobby Jones. Note sitting action for this No. 3 iron shot.

32

Bobby Locke (1959), a heavy-weight to-day, still manages to hit from inside to out. Note how his left hand is closing the club-face as he rolls his right shoulder but keeps his right arm bent. All Champions do this. Note the very closed stance — this suits some heavy-weights. (RIGHT): *Locke in 1938 — still the same action.*

Ed. ('Porky') Oliver weighs 220 pounds, but despite his bulk is one of the great golfers in America, capable of winning at any time.
  Here he is practising at White Sulphur Springs in 1956. His action is classical in every way. Note the way he holds the club-face square at impact with the side of his left hand; this is unusual but there, as always, is the bent right arm.

The late Aga Khan, a delightful person, and a keen golfer with little sartorial enthusiasm, found that with the left thumb outside, on this double-handed grip, he could get more rhythm in his shots. With extra weight, a privilege of age, his body action and footwork became slow, but that did not stop him from getting the maximum pleasure out of his regular game.

In his heydey a scratch golfer, Henry Longhurst, brilliant scribe and broadcaster, whom the fleeting years have made thicker-and-thicker-set, always wanted a little more freedom to make golf easy.
  His compact build has been a good base for his excellent short game and from being a regular slicer he has at last a gentle hook on his tee shots. I hope it lasts!!

There must be a difference in the swings of these two golfers. Mario Gonzales from Brazil, 'the Walking Pencil' as he was called in 1948, had a hip action which could be called snake-like. He used it to get power and to hold the club-face open, as his grip was part of the beginning of a shut-faced club action.

Harry Lipman, of the sturdy figure, has the opposite problems — the problems of the short golfer with the extra weight on; his objective is to move more, not less, and to try to get some hip action into his swing to stop the shoulders doing too much. He should never stand still at the address, his feet should be 'alive', he should begin his swing back from a 'little dance'.

LEFT: *Double-jointed James Adams, pro. at Royal Mid-Surrey Golf Club, can do the most rhythmic full swing even with both feet flat on the ground. Although now a veteran he can still swing as fully and as smoothly as he ever did.*

CENTRE: *Thick-set, short, sturdy Lionel Hebert, U.S. Ryder Cup player, a successful player on the Tournament Circuit, stands very near to the ball for his short shots. He is really 'crowding the ball'. I find this is a personal position — it looks cramped to me. Many would shank the ball from here.*

RIGHT: *The shoulders here work horizontally instead of under the head — the head has moved far to the right, throwing the whole swing off balance, and the bent right leg stops the swing from ever being firm. This closed club-face position and crumpled-up backswing make it difficult to stay on the 'inside of the ball'. This golfer does not use his height, and the ball is generally cut miserably. The real golf muscles are missing — that is why this happens.*

not enough hours of daylight in the day for me, I found I had to have a practice set and a 'best' set — a bit like the everyday suit and the Sunday suit.

This alone may have saved the backs of many players, but I am now of the opinion that if contra-exercises are done all along while practising — stretching exercises particularly — the human body is flexible enough to take the toughest punishment.

I have landed on daily stretching in the easy way, by using a telescopic expanding gym. bar which I fit in a door frame and take everywhere I go. After any spell in a slumped-up position, such as happens when reading, writing or golfing, just a few seconds of hanging seem to get my muscles all rested and relaxed again and strengthen my back.

After fifty years of age, it is not a question of looking for much improvement in one's physical condition. One is grateful if one can hold one's own, as it were. Golf is a great game, an ideal relaxation for all, but played incorrectly it can become tiring and can at odd times put a big strain on certain sectors of the body. The lower part of the spine and the left elbow are the two vulnerable points in the golfer, I have found from my experience as player and teacher.

Teaching, as I do, that golf is a game of the hands and arms where the club is swung and the body is almost encouraged to follow, I feel that I am guiding my pupils as far away as possible from physical damage. But when the player wants to

hit full o
shot, the
get good
strains.

You s
under to
the finge
is hit ou
If there
knees a
and sav
spikes h
spike ir
to actua
spikes
for they

If yo
that yo
your m
game –
consult
profess
advant
stretch
how t
stop t
provec
try to
youth

VERY OPEN TO SHUT

*Norman Drew, a promising North of Ireland professional
method'. This particular action originates in the grip (photo
by the camera at its 'shuttest'. In the third photograph he h
clubhead to make sure the face will be square at impact.
strain put on the spine. This is why I contend that this is only*

LEFT: *A thick-set veteran lady golfer, Mrs J. Hagander, gets well away from the ball at the address and uses a wide stance to get a solid whack at the ball. She remembers, too, to look at the ball with her left eye, which helps the backswing and the 'looking at the ball.'*

RIGHT: *Heavyweight W. J. ('Bill') Cox blasts his ball from powdery sand, cutting across the ball as he crashes into the sand behind the ball.*

for this, just as much as his rubber-jointed body. Peter Thomson, like most players who have grown up with steel shafts, punches the ball more — his swing is commercially efficient as opposed to Jones's wonderfully elegant action — but Thomson is of a more stocky build. Of our pros., Eric Brown has an ideal build — Peter Alliss, Bernard Hunt and David Thomas have the problems of the tall golfers to solve. Peter Alliss finds the mystery of the short game still his biggest problem — his natural arc is too wide. His father, Percy, a

beautiful player at his best, was the ideal build, I thought, and few players have ever been more machine-like through the green. Little Australian Norman Von Nida had a fine free action, with his fingers being very active during his swing. He had much success over here just after the war.

These few examples at random should give golfers reason to think about their own physique relative to what they are trying to do. There are particular actions which suit each player best. Have you found yours?

BALL IN THE CENTRE

This is how I like to begin my backswing for any full shot. Here I am playing a No. 3 iron shot — wide stance, ball off the centre. There is no doubt here that the left side is playing its part in pushing the club away from the ball, as the left knee is working inwards towards the ball.

OH, MY ACHING BACK!

CONTORTIONISTS ... SLIPPED DISCS .

| *Cary Middlecoff* | *Sam Snead* |

THERE is a lot of strain in the golf game. The need for the highest degree of mental concentration over an extended period of time 'kills off the giants even more quickly than the physical strain of wielding a club at a great speed, with the body twisted because the right hand fits below the left.

If the hands completely overlapped one over the other, the game would be easier, because the shoulders would then be level. But while this i possible physically, from a point of applying maximum power and control it would be useless.

Just look at the photograph of Cary Middleco finishing his swing. Everything is twisted from th ankles to the neck, and it needs an extra stron supple body to stand this strain, not only whe playing a round but also in the continual practi ing. In an actual round a player of Middlecof power would play only very few full shots wi any chosen club, but it is the hours on the practi tee which will take their toll unless contra-corrective exercises of some sort are done.

The fact that Sam Snead's game is so smoc and yet so strong is due to his magnificent pl sique. He does regular exercises night and mo ing. The man from the mountains of Virginia long realised that physical fitness pays off.

Just look at those arms! Slamming Sam 'arms like legs' and two hundred exercises a (with a spring-grip, with each arm) keep them this.

It is all very well to say 'sweep the ball aw But no golf ball was ever sent a long way with some sort of resistance creeping into the swin without hitting past the body and allowing

'Doing the bridge' in 1946, aged 39 — just checked up to see if I could do these exercises today and found I still could, but as it is a bit of a strain, I desist — I think wisely. There are other exercises less strenuous, such as swinging a heavy club, skipping and hanging, but I can still do this for a bet.

TAKE MY TIP AND KEEP FIT - EVEN AT 50!

MUCH as I dislike reminding myself that I am past 50, the grey hairs and the wrinkles are there. I cannot miss them. But I am beginning to realize that while a lot is past, there may still be much to come. And I am satisfied that the period from 30 to 50 is the most important of one's life in forming good health and exercise patterns. For most of us they are the busy years. And they pass all too quickly. But they are also the years during which a sane physical fitness programme must be followed if later life is to be enjoyed usefully.

After 30 most people are interested in economic or social success. And, not having the excess energy of the 20's, they rapidly deteriorate physically unless an intelligent balance is arrived at between work, feeding, resting and exercise. In other words, a great many people find it a lot easier to make a living than to *live*.

Most business men neglect exercise except at the week-end, when it is often too exhausting to do any good, while the womenfolk get thoroughly fatigued by the daily care of the house and children. In fact many men arrive at the office or works on Monday tired out after a week-end on the links or the tennis court, in the garden, or driving the car on crowded roads.

All this week-end 'living-it-up' can be mentally diverting, but from a health standpoint it's just dissipation. That's why I think the 30's to 50's are the years in which we must learn to *regulate* our

 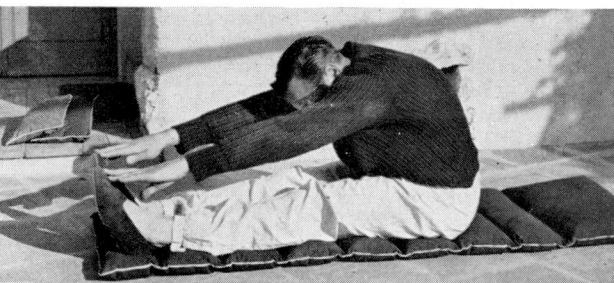 

I spent ten weeks that winter doing P.T. I can still do all this!

I have a portable gym bar.   *I won the Dunlop five rounds event by five strokes.*

energy. If one has been physically very active during the 20's, it is important to maintain most of this capacity as the 30's are reached.

Athletes who keep up their exercises have a longer life expectancy than non-athletes. Even those who neglect training for a spell can gradually work to a peak of physical fitness that gives the maximum functioning of the body for daily living. If you take my tip and decide to get yourself into the best possible shape for your age, you must have a medical check-up first. When did you last have one? Or are you one of those people who say 'Never had a doctor in my life'? Such people often go the quickest, remember. I've learned a lot from bitter experience. I wouldn't make the same mistakes again, but we get no second chances. There is just time, sometimes, to correct part of the errors.

When I decided to retire from big-time golf in 1948 and just play the rôle of spectator (almost business man-golfer you might call it) I found not only that my game deteriorated, the competitive edge being absent, but also that my design for living was missing. That is, there was no incentive to keep me in peak condition.

I stuck it out till 1952, making only a few mediocre shows in tournaments. But after Christmas, 1952 (I was rising 46), I thought I would have another big try just to see how much skill I had lost and how good the others who had taken my place were.

I spent ten weeks of that winter doing physical training exercises with an instructor who got me out of bed at 8 a.m. no matter how tired I was — and I *was* tired — playing and practising golf daily and carrying on with my usual social and business life.

By the end of April I had really toughened up.

The first event I played in I won easily, and I felt that my efforts and sacrifices had been worth while. But I had forgotten my age, in the excitement, and played in another big tournament two weeks later.

I did well, but not as well as in the first one. Then I tried a third. And when the ground began to heave like an ocean swell I guessed something was wrong. So it was that in June, 1953, I was pushed off to rest in France, for my heart was tired. I had done too much.

'No more big golf this year, my boy, and thereafter just a few events a year is your quota', said the doctor. I got a wigging from the Press for not playing in the Ryder Cup match at Wentworth (that October) which we nearly won, but was forbidden by Lord Evans, the famous physician, to put myself under great strain so soon.

All got well again. The heart rested up and the latest news (1959) is that it is better than at any time for years, but I must not overdo things.

I think I am best when I stick to my old pattern of keeping as fit as possible for coming tournaments. Though I play only a few now, they keep me trying, and this incentive is sufficient to make me keep in good general shape.

But it is no use expecting most middle-aged men and women to take time off each day to get down on the mat and do their daily dozen.

They all know they should. They all know they feel better for it. But it requires an abnormal amount of will-power, and too many drift along thinking they are fit.

What is the answer?

I have found that a few seconds at a time of s-t-r-e-t-c-h-i-n-g is just enough to keep one in shape.

I find it corrects the usually slumping postures we settle into during most of our day, and the natural extending of the spine acts as a relief as well as toughening up the all-important back muscles, and golfing muscles in particular, for those engaging in the sport.

Most people slump and slouch. And this poor posture contributes to all forms of ill health.

I have been hanging on the tops of door frames all my life — but you need very strong fingers for this, and besides the tops of door frames are always dirty. That is why the simple gym. bar is the thing. I have one in my luggage everywhere I go. I use one at home, on a ship, in hotel rooms.

Take my tip. Learn from my experience.

You must be fit to enjoy life. Just look around you. How many of your friends are really fit, how many try to keep in shape by diet and exercises? The answer, I'll bet, is a handful only.

The rest just let themselves go in the years from 30 to 50 in what I call the constructive years, too. Then they live (if they live on) to regret it.

So start stretching to-day. You'll never be sorry.

A TYPE OF PITCH

Tony Holguin, a pro. on the circuit in America, is seen here practising pitch shots (watched by Frank Stranahan and 'Toots', right. He is using a stiff-wristed action with lots of body as can be seen by the way he has finished this short stroke.

The wrists, the right especially, are locked at the top of the back swing and never move throughout the stroke; the knees and hips supply any flexibility in this action, passing through the ball.

TALKING ON THE COURSE

Some players keep relaxed through chatting as they go round, but I have found that I do play better if I concentrate to the maximum, and that means talking little and getting on with the job.

We all know the breezy type who tries to talk you out of it, and often does. He could be reminded of the saying of the old Scotsman who said: 'Golf is a game to be enjoyed or endured in silence.'

PRACTISING

WHETHER one practises a little or much depends on individual taste, but to practise regularly and frequently is a 'must' for everyone who wants to be good. Few golfers have remained great without regular practice, and none has arrived at being great without much practice.

Some players are gluttons for practice. One who comes to mind is Ben Hogan — he felt that 2½ hours was a sort of daily warming-up drill. I wonder what some of the giants of the past would think of this for a spell of hard labour. I have felt, as I have grown older, that it is only necessary to play 'like mad' when one is learning to play, but once a swing 'that works' has been acquired, then it is enough to keep the muscles toned up and to check on direction by hitting a certain number of balls.

Another American who is a slaving practiser is Frank Stranahan. I have studied him while practising, and after reaching a peak when he hit very many perfect shots in succession, he often continued to play on enthusiastically and then gradually passed this peak, and became tired. He then spent the rest of his time on the practice-ground correcting faults caused by the fatigue, which produced faults which were never really his normal errors. This sort of practice, except that it passes the time, is not really as beneficial as it should be. The time to stop is when you have the feeling that all is going well.

Every player has his own formula for practice. Some work hard on the short game, others only enjoy hitting full shots. Francis Ouimet once wrote that the best way to improve was to practise your best shots the most, and there are many golfers who support this theory. If perfection in putting was achieved in direct proportion to the hours practised, it would be only necessary to 'clock' a lot of time to be superlative, but, alas, the best putters often practise the least.

I have putting 'secrets' sent to me regularly; tapes on the ground, tape on the clubhead — one travels along the other — mirrors or reflectors or guides for the pendulum stroke, but these 'stunts' rarely make a bad putter into a Locke.

I do not say they do not work at all, because this is not true. Someone has usually benefited from the invention, but the really good putter is born, I am satisfied. Practising on the putting green for sixpence a putt — that means trying on every single putt — is by far the best method of improving. Laying dozens of balls down and putting them one after the other is a way of getting the touch of the green, but the stroke, while it can be claimed it becomes mechanical, does not tax the co-ordination, for it becomes too automatic from a distance-judging point of view, and ball after ball is sent to the hole side from habit, not from the direct orders of the delicate distance-controlling mechanism of the body.

I still love practising, and while I always have a sort of regret at cutting-up lovely close-knit turf, it is, of course, the only way to expect to play iron shots consistently. I recall a single-figure handicap golfing friend of mine ruining his short game, through playing up and down his perfect tennis lawn without taking a divot. He developed a frightened sort of half-topped stroke which was very difficult to cure. 'Cut up your lawn', I said, 'You never play tennis, and besides, the gardener can always re-turf it.' It never happened, and he went on half-topping.

If you set out to hit a lot of balls and you are not used to this training, put on a left-hand glove, which fits tightly, *before* your hand gets sore. Once you have the slightest sign of a blister, stop!

I think it is a good idea to hit the full shots while you are fresh, as at the beginning of a practice session, and finish on the shorter ones.

Fit in some practice using each hand separately, but once the hand and arm tire, change over and give it a rest. Do not hesitate to try out extremes in stances and grips — it is the only way to learn about golf.

Dai Rees practising putting with a long row of balls lined up ready for striking.

THEY ALL PRACTISE

LEFT: *A scene by the score-board at the Seminole Club, Florida, U.S.A., during a lunch-time break at a tournament. Dozens of bags of practice balls belonging to the professionals lie around unguarded, which makes one think the Americans must be very honest people, leaving such treasures about!*

RIGHT: *A few minutes later, after the players have had a light lunch, the practice-ground is crowded again. Walter Burkemo and Billy Maxwell are in the foreground.*

LEFT: *1958 U.S. Open Champion, Tommy Bolt, practising. Note the way his left hand and arm are working. While there is a 'climb over' right over left, there is no sign of collapse by the left; it is still guiding the club, elbow down.*

CENTRE: *Dick Mayer practising in May, 1957. Mayer became U.S. Open Champion a month later, and then won the 50,000 dollar prize in Chicago that August. Note left hand and open club-face.*

RIGHT: *Sam Snead playing 30-yard pitches to a green. Note how firmly these shots are played — no slackening of the grip or arm muscles, and what arms! Sam does not flick the ball; he has no need to do so, anyhow, and, secondly, he prefers to go slowly 'through the ball'. Note also the practice balls are opposite the right toe.*

LEARN TO MOVE

Holding the shoulders steady by placing the hands on the top of the club and then working the hips quickly from left to right is a good exercise. This can be done anywhere, but a little daily drill in the door-frame of the bathroom is perhaps the best place to give the muscles of the back, midriff and legs a beneficial work-out. The knees are pushed in towards the ball (left-right, left-right) repeatedly.

CHECK YOUR LEFT ARM AND GRIP

LEFT: *This is the only way to find out exactly how good your left arm really is and if it could respond to any demand to play a bigger part in the swing if called upon. Most handicap golfers find this very difficult to do. Good golfers can hit balls quite readily, even if they have never done it before. Here Spanish Amateur Champion, Mr A. Maura, is trying one-armed shots for the first time. The young caddie seems to be unconsciously expressing doubts about his master's ability to do it, judging by his pose.*

RIGHT: *In this swing the left arm has not played its best rôle in the swing, for the elbow has bent. This action can be used to ensure that the club-face is held open, as in 'cutting the ball', but it is a weak action and here the ball was definitely pushed, not whipped. Compare this left arm action with that of Tommy Bolt on the opposite page, where the elbow points down.*

43

ANOTHER PAIL OF BALLS GONE

Myself practising at the Piping Rock Club, Long Island, U.S.A. Note size of practice-ground — actually two full-size adjoining polo fields — which must form the biggest practice-ground in the world. I am overlapping two fingers of the right hand on the left at this moment.

CHECK YOUR RIGHT ARM AND GRIP

One-handed practice is hard to beat as a strengthener for the grip and arm. Here is a young man, who is almost a scratch golfer, showing a perfect right-handed action. This requires a lot of strength and control. He hit the ball very well and this was the first time he had ever tried right hand alone.

ONE THING AT A TIME

A new golfer taking a lesson cannot just yet remember everything. He has kept his head down, but forgotten to move his feet properly or to hold his left arm firm. Here a bit of individual arm-drill can help things along faster, but it takes time to learn to strike a golf ball accurately. Professional giving lesson: H. Giraud of Mougins, Cannes.

LOOKING AT YOURSELF

Y<small>OU</small> look at yourself daily in a glass but, of course, the reflection is the 'wrong way round', so that when a player tries to analyse his swing before a mirror it is as though a left-handed player was standing facing him and playing the same way. This is the way a teacher sees his pupil. The Duke of Gramont invented an apparatus which corrected this situation, so that on looking into a mirror the golfer could see himself the 'right way round'. It was a bulky apparatus, and so was never a commercial success, but the idea appealed to me.

It is just this difference which makes it tricky to analyse one's swing: we do not always have the gift 'to see oursel's as others see us'.

I have never quite arrived, even after all these years, at being able to know *exactly* what I am doing; photographs and cine-strips have helped me, of course, but it is rarely possible to know exactly what happened in any one particular stroke, in actual play, unless a slow-motion camera was working.

One thing a golfer *can* check on readily is how his hands look viewed from above and how they look when he turns his head to the right to see the top of his back swing. He knows just how *his* hands look, but rarely does he get the chance to see what other players see when they look at their hands in these same positions.

I got Hilaire Giraud, the French professional at Cannes, to photograph my hands as I see them, getting him to hold the camera near enough to my normal eye position. Because my head took up the exact place the camera should have been occupying,

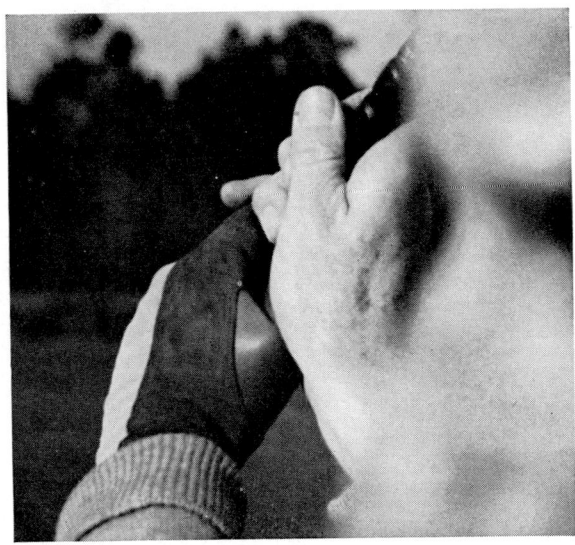

Looking at the grip from the front of the face at eye level.

the picture of the hands at the address position, viewed from above, was taken from the right side of my head and shows the right hand looking very much more over the club than it actually is; and the photograph of the hands at the top of the back swing is taken from just before my head, so again the camera does not quite view the position 'from my eyes'. Still it gives an idea and any keen student can get his hands so photographed and make a comparison.

When teaching golf, instructors very often do imitations of their pupils, staging the exact position at address or throughout the swing, in an endeavour 'to paint a picture' the pupil can remember. '*Oh, am I doing that?*' is the sort of surprised comment by a pupil on seeing more or less what he is doing — or failing to do.

During the past few years I have been working on my own swing to get the club, if possible, more upright, as I think with age one's swing gets flatter. I decided I had been going too much around my body, and when I asked just how upright was the last swing I had made, I found it difficult to believe it had moved so little from its old track, and yet it felt as if it had gone up over my head. Only a demonstration by Giraud convinced me that I was not swinging where I wanted to get! It has moved but little, despite my efforts.

The photograph of the hands at the address shows how the big muscle of the right thumb becomes prominent as the shaft is squeezed between the finger and thumb of this hand. This never shows so clearly from any other angle. The 'V' can

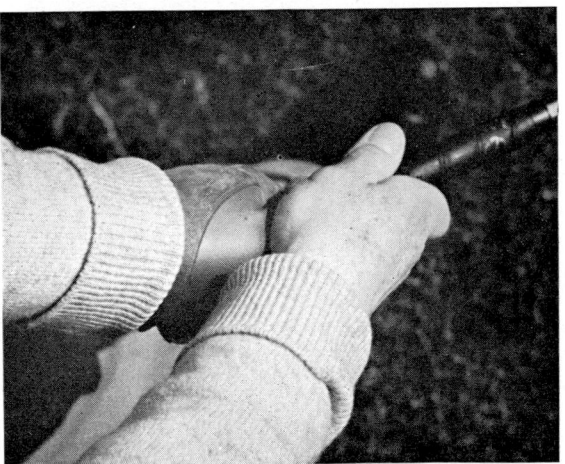

Looking over my right shoulder — this is how my hands appear. Note muscle of right thumb.

be seen pointing up the shaft, and the back of the gloved left hand is towards the hole.

In the 'top of the back swing' photograph, a pose which makes the swing short, the exact angle from which the photograph is seen by my eyes, the grip with the right hand 'club-shaft in the fingers' is clear.

So often I find golfers thinking the ball is, say, opposite the left heel when it is near the centre of the feet; just a slight step away with the right foot (as Fred Daly does) before beginning the back swing 'moves' the ball effectively, nearer to the left foot. I often wonder if Fred Daly began this trick or mannerism to get as far behind the ball as possible, or just to get his back swing started smoothly.

I find that the position of the club-face at address, especially with iron clubs — viz., open, square or closed — is always a problem, because it looks so very different from a spectator's position in front. I can get this problem straightened out with a mirror before the pupil, or by holding the club-face carefully to the ball, taking up the pupil's stance, and then asking him to take my place in front, and so see himself as another sees him.

Another point which is hard to 'see' is whether the hands are in line with the shaft or ahead of it at address; few players set their hands behind the ball. I have seen Hogan with his hands behind at the address, even for iron clubs. He claims it does away with the need for a forward press. It might be so for his game, but I know that experienced teachers would never dare to encourage it.

For most players the hands are in an ideal position when they are just slightly ahead at the address. This seems to encourage late hitting and a cocking of the wrists, and goes with a three-knuckle grip, as the left hand is set more to 'a back to the hole' position.

All the positions referred to in these notes are, in the end, personal ones, because they refer to the minor adjustments players make from time to time — but the whole point of 'Looking at Oneself' is to get the proportions right, and not to exaggerate.

A COMPARISON IN THE PITCH SHOT

Here are two photographs of the same shot, one played by Harry Vardon and the other by myself. The actions are almost identical, and the ball curiously enough has just reached the same spot in its flight to the pin.

There is the same easing of the knees and the steady head, while there is every indication that the shot has been played without the huge divots so common to-day in the play of many golfers, but really not necessary unless the lie is very tight. In my golfing costume, the bent right arm can be noted even at this point of the swing.

A COMPARISON WITH HOGAN

*Here is an opportunity to compare the back swing of Ben [...]
the very top of my back swing — Ben generally allows his [...]
could not be more alike, viewed from this angle.*

*The angles of the legs, the right arm and wrist position [...]
than I do to-day — he is slimmer anyway — and so unwind [...]*

TELEVISION SHOT AND PUTT

In my book, 'This Game of Golf', is a photograph of myself playing a 'shot in a million' from the face of the bunker on the right-hand side of the 8th green at Sandwich in the 1934 Open. Here I am re-creating the scene for B.B.C. Television. It took some three hours on a cold December day to play this shot over again.

Here I am in position ready to attack the ball, which is plugged and almost buried overhead in the sandy face, just as it was all those years ago. I got the ball out on to the green in 1934 and with two putts collected a fortunate 4. I went on to do a 65 — still a championship record.

On the 11th green at the Temple Golf Club, Maidenhead, doing a putt for the television camera, when I made a series for the B.B.C. on golf. I am using my old square-shafted putter which I have had since 1936.

A LITTLE DIFFERENCE WITH A BIG DIFFERENCE

LEFT: *I am addressing the ball for a No. 2 iron shot with my hands slightly ahead of the ball. This, I find, makes me cock my wrists earlier and tends to keep much more weight on the left foot at the top of the back swing.*

RIGHT: *I have set my hands behind the ball. This seems to go with a wider arc in the back swing.*

These little differences creep into everybody's game and can have quite a big effect on the results. They are hard to detect, and that is why it is always good to have someone around, who understands your game, to ask. Do you mean to do this or that? Why not get the camera out and get something to study on paper.

This stance is narrower than I use for my big iron shots normally. I was just posing to show the differences.

D

TWENTY YEARS BETWEEN

Twenty
(they
grows
two ph
the d
really.
seem
otherw
altered

NO INVENTION OF MINE

I am not inventing this grip you see — it was used years ago. This photograph of the golfer on the course shows a similar grip — the photograph dates from 1900.

I do not like it, but it can be used, and the old golfer on the right, Horace G. Hutchinson, was a champion — so it works. If the accepted orthodox grip does not produce results, why not try it? After all, golf is a game where the control of the finger tension is 'the great secret'.

TAKING AIM

Some players have been taught to stand behind the ball and point the club at the target as a means of impressing on themselves where they are going. Personally I have never seen the point of this, but never despise any such tips. Try anything, they say, once! This pupil of mine, Mme E. Visser, picked this tip up while golfing on the continent. I did not teach it; in fact, I do not see the value of it. But if it helps, why not?

THIS AIMING BUSINESS

ONE of the most difficult parts of the golf game for the beginner, once he has a reasonably consistent impact, is to aim his shot. This problem can be solved only on a golf course, and then really only on the practice ground. The value of learning the swing indoors in the initial stages of becoming acquainted with golf shows up to advantage, in my opinion, against beginning on the course, because the pupil becomes conscious of his swing and does not worry about where the ball goes. The extra problem at the beginning of 'why did that one go there'? — a question that cannot continually be passed over by 'Don't worry about that yet!' — wastes so much time and energy, during the first lessons, that much faster progress is made playing into nets, for the player can concentrate on the job in hand: that of swinging the club smoothly.

Once a pupil has got a sound, grooved swing and *can hold on to the club at impact*, the direction of the shot, which comes mainly from the correct placing of the body, can be acquired readily. This does not mean that the stance or the taking of aim is learned for good, for a trip round the championships will show players of the calibre of Snead, Stranahan, Hogan and Player, etc., playing endless shots on the practice-ground, some with a club lying touching their toes and pointing in the direction they wish the shot to go. They thus check up on their aim in this way.

I begin with my pupils by teaching them to stand with their toes parallel one to the other, and the lines across the toes parallel to the line ball-to-hole; and for a drive, with the ball on the inside of the left foot. This is just a simple programme to follow at the start. All sorts of adjustments come later as the player develops, these being made necessary by his own physical make-up.

The stance is important for two main reasons: it is the position of the feet from which the player intends to strike the ball, and it is responsible in the main for the aiming of the stroke.

Experienced players know that the hands have the final say, if they are strong and trained, for a club-face impact angle can be corrected sometimes if a faulty body action is leading it to the ball not in the position initially conceived; but to most golfers to aim wrongly, or to swing wrongly, means a misdirected shot. No players, of course, quite agree on what percentage the body plays in the swing, but that it has to aim the ball is generally accepted.

A club laid on the ground will help in aiming.

Abe Mitchell and George Duncan both impressed me as a young player by the way they seemed to fall into place, once they got up to the ball. There was no shuffling about, no fidgety movements. They gripped the club, put it behind the ball, and seemed then to line up to the hole, not to the ball.

Many of my readers will have read at one time or another the interesting test some of Harry Vardon's friends carried out when in search of 'why the Old Master was so devastatingly consistent?' Why were his shots so straight? They could have been fired from a gun. Did he have the knack of always finding exactly the same stance each time? Tests proved that in six consecutive perfect drives, with the ball always teed in the same place, and the ball driven between two trees, he had a slightly different foot position each time.

What does this prove, if anything? He was able to make all the necessary adjustments during each swing to ensure that the ball flew in the direction he had selected. Of course Harry Vardon was precise. He had a sense of 'where the ball was' that was exceptional.

Harry Weetman tries the harness for pitching. This strapping of the elbows to the body teaches footwork and body action in the shorter shots.

causing the player to repeat his best swing with almost monotonous regularity, do make a golfer aiming-conscious, as the rolling shoulder action of the body almost disappears and the arms go on, extended, to the hole.

All the same, most players do not pivot enough on the backswing, and although Bobby Locke has by no means a classical action — he exaggerates his closed stance — he is one player who really gets his back to the hole at the top of every swing; and this happens with him even for quite short shots. This is possible because at address his left shoulder points to 'long off' if not to 'mid-off', 30° right of the target, i.e., well to the right of the flag.

The left shoulder being well forward does help pivoting, and I think helps aiming, despite the fact that the open stance is universally recommended by instructors.

When a real beginner first plays on the course, he almost needs to be told at every shot how to aim, how to adjust his aiming; and that means how to stand to the ball. Someone has to tell him, for it is one of the most difficult things to adjust alone, for 'you cannot see yourself', and it is too late once the shot has gone.

One of his favourite tricks was to place a ball in the outside twigs of a small bush at a sufficient height from the ground to be able to get under the ball with a driver swing, and then hit the ball vertically up into the air as high as he could; and this would be done with his small-headed, shallow-faced driver, too. I have in my possession one of the actual clubs he would use for this trick. If you have any doubts about the skill required to do this shot, please try it next time you pass a suitable bush.

Getting back to this taking aim question, I recommend pupils to point the left shoulder at the hole and to hit towards the ball from the inside; for the long shots, that is. A narrower, open stance, where the hips partially face the hole, is best, perhaps, for the shorter shots, as in these more easily-performed strokes the body is best put out of the way. The arms and hands alone guide the ball to the pin. Some modern power players use shoulders and stomach for approaching — too much action, I think, for a small shot.

You may remember my advising golfers to try the harness and the swing-moulder idea, which holds the elbows together. Well, these straps,

Bobby Locke gets his back to the hole at the top of every swing. Here he is half-way back. Note how already his shoulders are well round — left shoulder pointing at the ball.

AIMING TIPS

On taking aim — left shoulder forward and high. Most low-handicap golfers look over their left shoulder, at the address, to the target for full shots. Point the left shoulder at the target, or to the right of it, is a good tip.

Note Henri de Lamaze, H. Archibald of Paris and myself all follow this plan when taking aim.

PRACTISE CAREFULLY

This golfer had every intention of playing for the caddie, but stood carelessly, and so the ball finished well wide of the mark.

ON TAKING AIM: A DETAIL

Some golfers do better when they aim their feet at the hole, even for putting (2), others prefer the parallel stance as in (1). The main thing is to know what you are trying to do. Abe Mitchell told me, when I was a young professional and sat at the feet of this great striker, that he stood to the hole often in preference to standing to the ball and then 'aiming his stance'. Great golfers usually 'fall into their stance', they rarely shuffle about. Years of practice have done this, it is not a gift.

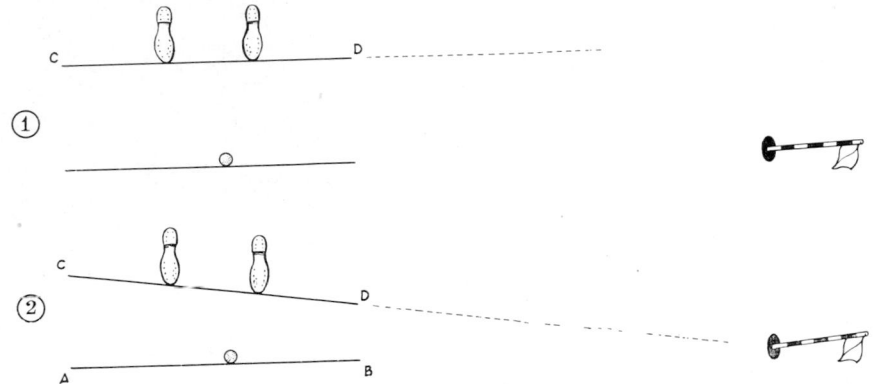

ON OVERSWINGING

One of the best brakes on overswinging is a tight-fitting jacket — but I have yet to see a golfer, male or female, of the present epoch who gets the club hanging down the back, who would ever bother to try this idea out. I can mention in passing that Abe Mitchell, one of my boyhood heroes, preferred a tight-fitting jacket for golf; he felt his swing was always under control.

REMEMBER

The imaginary line to the hole — the clubhead stays on the line only a short time, but you must force the clubhead to follow along it. Put a peg tee six inches ahead of the ball and try to knock it down with your follow through.

Iᴛ is, of course, accepted th
game, and except in the c
left-handed, or those odd
with the hands crossed, as i
is always below the left.

Most golfers, and I clai
can swing the club with a l
with their left hand only. Pe
strength and precision, but
sort of abandon which the r
has, and can never get.

The left arm hanging free
with a golf club at the end o
ation of the arm as it were
shoulder-joint like a windn
right hand on the shaft and
This is inevitable in a way, b
arm-plus-club, while still tryi
left shoulder-joint, has a s
which interferes with its fre
reason is that now, if we take
one unit, then half-way do
radius, shoulder to clubhead
a guide, ready to help the fr
to propel the dead weight of
object of the game is to hit t
direction and to a certain
wishing we had no right l
because we should make a v
left hand only business.

Teachers and players of t
showing pupils, and convinc
how the left arm works; and
this arm, hoping to develop
But however much they atte
manner in which it works,
ways be at the mercy of the
especially under pressure, or v
as all players like to do.

I stress the right hand imp
even the very positioning of t
ignoring the fact that a tens
affect the swing, can alter th
left arm swings' or wants to
if uneducated entirely, ruin a
the left arm.

It is clear that the influenc
halfway down the length of th
clubhead, must be dominant
best will in the world, nothi
unless the right hand and a
play their precise rôle.

So, when one talks of lef

JUDGING THE LAG

THE SECRET OF TIMING

Fᴇᴡ handicap golfers, endeavouring to emulate their favourite star player by delaying the hit, really realize what it means. They try to get into a late hit position without having any hit to offer. I have chosen an old photograph, this time of Lawson Little, a wonderful golfer of pre-war days, who had the right fighting spirit and a dashing sort of game to go with it. Lawson always attacked the ball as though it were his worst enemy, and before the arrival of the fourteen-club rule he sometimes carried — or rather his caddie did — 24 clubs, including a veritable battery of pitching clubs.

SHUT-FACED ACTION

Lawson, like most long hitters, was at times wild off the tee, and as he used a more shut than open club-faced action, he needed to stay well behind the ball, to knock it up, as it were, for his wooden shots.

Here he is seen to have set his body ready to hit the ball in the back and while the clubhead is already moving fast — I estimate it will reach its maximum speed at the point marked X — it should be noted that the hands will scarcely advance at all until after impact; the clubhead will, in fact, overtake them. The dotted line shows where the arms and shaft will be in line at impact.

While there is no doubt that 'Swing the Club-head' is an ideal slogan, in a basic way, once the question of applying the maximum power comes in, then, as this photograph shows, there is some evidence of the lever principle appearing. Lawson Little, like all top golfers, will not straighten his right arm till after impact.

WIDE STANCE

Another point which I recommend all golfers to study is the wonderfully wide base from which Lawson directs his operation. Not for him the narrow squatting sort of pose, but a wide, manly, solid width, in which he can use his feet and legs to the best advantage. Here is the hit past the chin de luxe; the braced left leg and the thrust with the right leg. His rolling on to the outside edge of his left shoe is typical of the way this foot often works when the big hitters let fly! In fact, many have been photographed while on the toes of both feet.

I find that very many what one might call ordinary golfers never realize, throughout the whole of their golfing life, that there is a sort of time-lag

in executing the commands ordered by the brain to the clubhead. That when the brain says, *now apply the power,* it is often too late to time the ball, and furthermore, in the great haste to give the maximum, the muscles nearer the headquarters of command react first — the shoulders, for example — and so throw everything out of line, including the arc of the swing.

SENSE OF TIMING

Children handling golf clubs from their earliest days instinctively assess this time-lag, and so grow

I think this photograph of Lawson Little (one of America's great golfers in pre-war years) is very instructive as it shows Lawson (in this younger days a colossal hitter) getting at the ball 'from behind'.

He has braced his body, his left leg is straight, his hips fully turned ready to flash the club at the ball. His shoulders are rotating under the head and the right arm will not straighten till after impact, but golfers must remember that already the clubhead is nearly at its maximum speed, which will be reached at the point X — *before the ball, not at the ball. So many golfers, when they try for length, lean into the ball and do not get to their maximum speed till too late.*

up with a natural s
I suppose, is all th
end. We call it wai
for it!' — giving th
by not letting any
too fast, too soon
in the execution of
ten tried on these c
are set up to test a
say, the brakes in a
appreciable; seven-
a good reaction.

ANTICIPATE T

It is perhaps nc
point which I have
is never easy to ant
it. That is why I l
with an X some tw
cause I have proved
anticipation is just e
hit in on time. Harr
his pupils aim an ir
to the green becaus

SNEAD AIM

*Sam Snead practisir
club, White Sulphur
how he stands to aim
Ben Hogan, practis
picks a club from hi
there is no doubt that
at the caddie. Photog
1948.*

YOUR CLUBS

Do not forget that t
power, and a weight r
which you will lose cc
The grip size is of v
Experiment! Better tc
celluloid ring at the bc
the old-fashioned stri
wrong thickness of har
Golf is a game of har

Stanley P. Morrison, a keen West of Scotland amateur, playing a perfect golf stroke. The right hand has come into the shot at the exact moment and the shoulders have not been displaced — they face squarely to the ball. If you can force a shot without your shoulders interfering you are already a golfer. Golfers who use their hands to this maximum as this golfer does, play past their body, not along with it.

determined to get to its place, near the right side, sooner almost than is necessary.

So when golf instructors say 'Let your left arm control the swing', they ought to add: 'If your right arm will allow it.' That is why an educated right arm is essential. Yet how many instructors teach their pupils how to use this arm and hand? It is often taken for granted, but it needs as much training as the left arm, because a golf swing is an unnatural action.

Older golfers will remember Irishman Jimmy Bruen, who really astounded the golfing world with his power and skill before the war. As a boy of from seventeen to nineteen years of age, he played fabulous shots, and really hit the ball like a 'horse kicking'. With his swing the clubhead went away up and finally forward, till it was almost over the ball at the very top of the back swing. Many old pros. prophesied that he would not be able to 'hit his hat' before long, with a swing like that. But the more I played with him the more I realized how sound it was, because he did everything right, only

'a bit more so'. He allowed the club to swing up freely, and as far as it wanted to go, the right hand just following passively until it was ready to give the ball that 'wicked whip' in the hitting area.

He had that gift of being able to swing the club as his left arm wanted, with no right arm interference, and few are the players who have even done that. I think his right shoulder-joint must have been extra mobile.

Jimmy Bruen damaged his right hand in 1940, and even to-day, after numerous surgical operations, he cannot hit a golf ball without great pain. This has been a great loss to golf, because he really contributed something worthwhile, and if he can stand the pain of the impact, he still 'knocks them a mile', with the same old swing which so many said would not work.

One teaching professional in America shows his pupils what he means by left arm control by scarcely touching the club-shaft with his right hand, only using it to steady the shaft at the top of the swing, but I know this pro. would be happier if he could arrive in the same position with his right hand placed normally on the shaft.

Showing Jimmy Bruen how the left hand goes through and the left leg resists — taken during a session together at Royal Mid-Surrey Golf Club, where I was professional from 1946–52. Note my 'back of the left hand to the hole' action, and Jimmy's thoughtful 'I used to do that' expression.

58

If the present general system of teaching golf was entirely sound, players would only need continual swinging of the club with left arm only to succeed, but while this arm forms the swing, it is powerless in most cases to carry out its intentions once the right hand is in position and begins to operate. Each player has his own problem to work out in the shape of his own body, and therefore the actual angle at which the right arm comes on to the shaft is important and needs to be studied.

One instructor states that 'the golfer who lets his right side overpower his left will rarely ever pro-

One-armed golfer, George A. Wilde, plays right-handed, fore-handed. I personally hit the ball less well this way, but can make a decent show when I get the arm warmed up. I find that when I try to play a round of golf with just one hand, I need to use my right hand fore-handed for all short shots and putting. I use my left hand for my big shots.

With Jimmy Nicholls, a one-armed American professional, who plays beautiful golf left-handed, back-handed. He can play around scratch, given suitable lies. Once he gets into trouble his results are bound to be affected. He puts on a fine exhibition, and his great shots often embarrass his two-armed colleagues. He has no right hand problems!

gress beyond the "fairly good" class', but as I have already said, it is a bit negative to think in this way — far better that the right arm be educated, because it cannot and must not be ignored to succeed. It has a major part to perform, an instinctive part, too — that of attacking the ball.

So do not think that endless swinging of the left arm is the answer to all problems; it helps, but watch the right arm, educate it.

HITTING AGAINST THE BACK OF THE LEFT HAND

The left hand and impact positions that handicap golfers seek; there is no club-slip here, beginners note.

THE FULL TOP

A top occurs because the clubhead makes contact with the ball above its centre.

Here is the end of a swing with the ball completely topped; the ball, which can be seen, in fact finished up only forty yards from the tee. The body has straightened up too soon, as the head has gone with the stroke, and with the ball. Where it is seen here, a mere ten yards from the spot on which it was teed, the head should still be down. I have seen it quoted that a full shot should travel at least thirty-five yards before the eye picks it up. Does this happen when you drive? A sort of 'Wait and See' is indicated, like "'it and 'ark' for putting.

BALL

LOOKING AT THE BALL

Alec Fox, one of our coming young professionals, really does look at the ball — ideal for him, but perhaps too long for some players, especially those of the wide-shouldered breed.

WATCH YOUR STANCE

This golfer either stood for a hook deliberately or took very poor aim. Her feet 'go' well to the right of the target — see arrow. This shot was mishit, so I could not quite judge, but the point that stands out is the way the hips have acted as a brake on the entire action. Clearly the shoulders have started the down swing, but the feet have not played any worthwhile part at all in this action, and the head has followed the ball! I am sure a spell playing barefooted would teach this golfer a lot.

FLAG